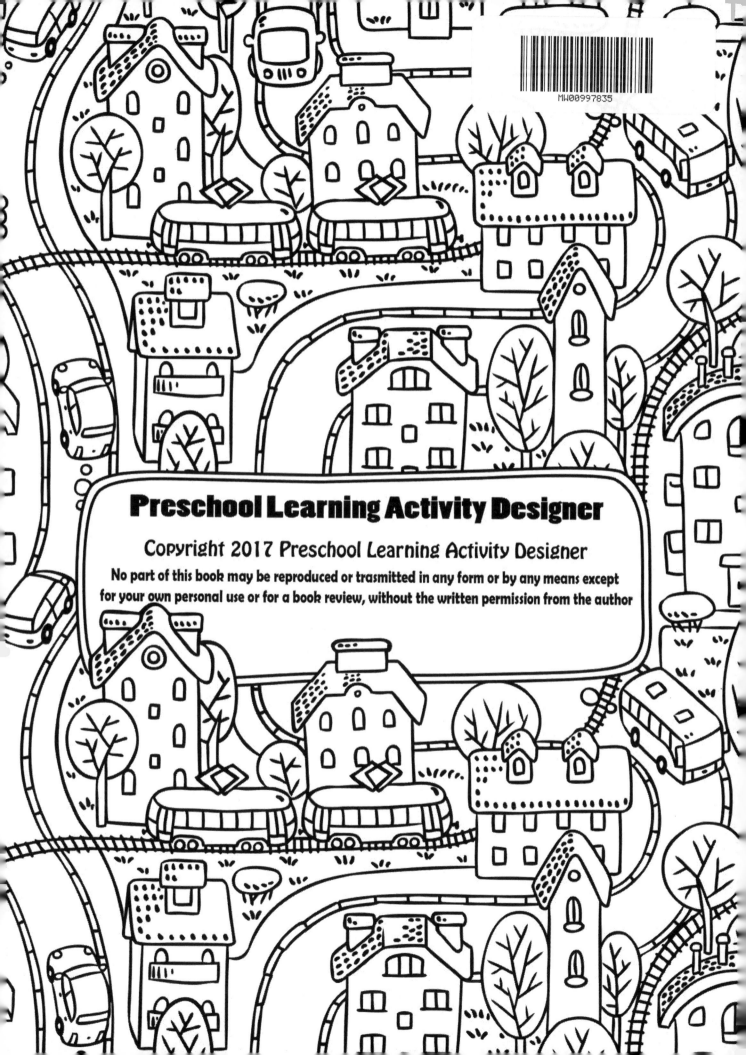

Preschool Learning Activity Designer

Copyright 2017 Preschool Learning Activity Designer

No part of this book may be reproduced or trasmitted in any form or by any means except for your own personal use or for a book review, without the written permission from the author

MW00997835

THIS BOOK BELONG TO

....

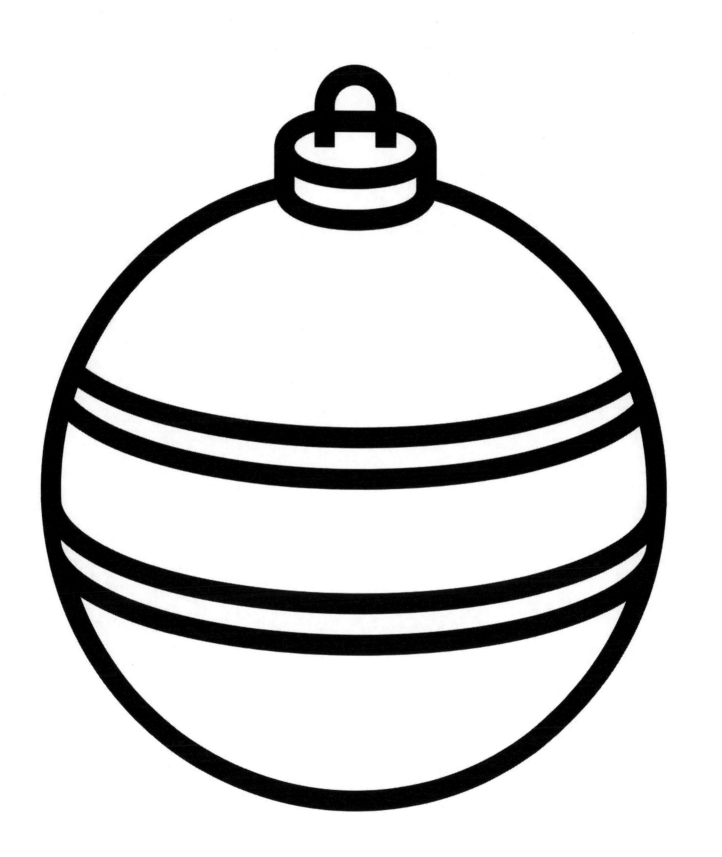

96921402R00035

Made in the USA
San Bernardino, CA
21 November 2018